Tucson
PERSPECTIVES

Schiffer Publishing Ltd®

4880 Lower Valley Road, Atglen, Pennsylvania 19310

Written and Photographed
by Scott D. Butcher

D1379322

Dedication

For Bernice "Mimi" Butcher

Contents

Other Schiffer Books by the Author:
Lancaster County Reflections, 978-0-7643-3584-6, $24.99
York: America's Historic Crossroads, 978-0-7643-3012-4, $29.99
Tombstone: Relive the Gunfight at the OK Corral, 978-0-7643-3425-2, $9.99
Delaware Reflections, 978-0-7643-3200-5, $29.99
Gettysburg Perspectives, 978-0-7643-3296-8, $9.99
Spooky York Pennsylvania, 978-0-7643-3021-6, $14.99

Other Schiffer Books on Related Subjects:
A Journey through Northern Arizona, 978-0-7643-3010-0, $24.99
A Journey through Southern Arizona, 978-0-7643-3269-2, $24.99

Copyright © 2011 by Scott D. Butcher
Unless otherwise noted, all images are the property of the author.
Library of Congress Control Number: 2011920269

Designed by Mark David Bowyer
Type set in Serifa BT / Souvenir Lt BT

ISBN: 978-0-7643-3712-3
Printed in China

Schiffer Books are available at special discounts for bulk purchases for sales promotions or premiums. Special editions, including personalized covers, corporate imprints, and excerpts can be created in large quantities for special needs. For more information contact the publisher:

Published by Schiffer Publishing Ltd.
4880 Lower Valley Road
Atglen, PA 19310
Phone: (610) 593-1777; Fax: (610) 593-2002
E-mail: Info@schifferbooks.com

For the largest selection of fine reference books on this and related subjects, please visit our website at:
www.schifferbooks.com
We are always looking for people to write books on new and related subjects. If you have an idea for a book please contact us at the above address.

This book may be purchased from the publisher.
Include $5.00 for shipping.
Please try your bookstore first.
You may write for a free catalog.

In Europe, Schiffer books are distributed by
Bushwood Books
6 Marksbury Ave.
Kew Gardens
Surrey TW9 4JF England
Phone: 44 (0) 20 8392 8585; Fax: 44 (0) 20 8392 9876
E-mail: info@bushwoodbooks.co.uk
Website: www.bushwoodbooks.co.uk

Introduction

Situated in the sprawling Sonoran Desert in a high desert valley along the banks of the Santa Cruz River, Tucson is Arizona's oldest city and one of the oldest continually-inhabited locations in the United States with evidence suggesting more than 10,000 years of human history. Tucson is a town of many names and a blend of many cultures. The word Tucson is based upon the Spanish name Tucsón (pronounced tuk-son), in turn based upon the O'odam name Cuk Son, which translates as "at the base of the black hill." The Old Pueblo is one of Tucson's best-known nicknames, named for the Presidio San Agustín del Tucsón, the Spanish garrison that was established in 1775. Moving from the past to the present, Tucson is also known as the Sunshine Factory, a nickname that embraces Tucson's reputation as one of the sunniest places in the United States — with an average of 350 sunny days a year. And from the present into the future, Tucson is also known as Optics Valley, named for the pioneering optics research at the University of Arizona, the prevalence of optics companies based here, and a number of notable astronomical observatories that search the planets and the stars — perhaps viewing worlds that mankind will visit one day in the distant future.

Tucson is also a melting pot of cultures. Her first inhabitants were Native Americans like the Hohokam, who lived in the region until the middle of the fifteenth century. The Tohono O'Odham (translated as People of the Desert), who trace their ancestry to the Hohokam, have occupied the Tucson area for centuries. Spanish Conquistadors arrived in southern Arizona in the mid-1500s, but the first permanent Spanish settlement did not occur until much later with the establishment of the Mission San Xavier del Bac in 1692 and construction of the Tubac Presidio in 1752. Though the Spanish Jesuit priests were able to make peace with the Tohono O'odam and convert many to Christianity, a series of battles occurred between Spain and Apache warriors in what became known as the Spanish-Apache Wars. Tucson was attacked by Apaches in 1779 and 1782. New Spain became part of Mexico in 1821 after an eleven-year war ended with Mexican independence, and Tucson added yet another layer to its history and culture. Thirty-two years later, in 1853, the Gadsden Purchase was completed and Tucson became part of the United States.

In the years that followed, Tucson served as the Western Capital of the Confederate Arizona Territory and Capital of the Arizona Territory from 1867 to 1877. The arrival of the railroad in 1880 and the discovery of silver in southern Arizona heralded in a new era for the desert community. So important was Tucson that the University of Arizona was established here in 1885, twenty-seven years before Arizona became a state. The Arizona State Museum was founded in Tucson by the Arizona Territorial Legislature in 1893. By the time John Dillinger arrived in 1934, selecting Tucson as a location to lay low from the FBI, the population was over 33,000 people.

The merging of cultures that Tucson has experienced since the sixteenth century is still happening today. The Mexican border is nearby, and over two million Mexicans annually visit the Tucson area. The Tohono O'Odham Reservation is located to the west and south of Tucson, and new residents from all over the United States — and beyond — are flocking to the region. Today over 540,000 people reside within the city while the greater metropolitan area, which comprises about 600 square miles, is home to over one million people. Contrast that with the Tucson population of 1900, when the dusty desert town was home to only about 7,500 residents. One of the fastest-growing cities in the United States, Tucson offers a temperate climate with a preponderance of sunshine, a picturesque setting amidst the desert floor yet surrounded by towering mountains, and a quality of life that promises a small-town feel with enough big-city amenities to keep one interested. Recognized by Business Week and the AARP as a best place to retire, Tucson is also a destination for retirees who live here year-round and "snowbirds" who winter in Tucson.

Framed by the Santa Catalina, Rincon, Tucson, Santa Rita, and Tortolita Mountains, Tucson is very much a town of the desert. Residents not only embrace this setting, they relish it: stucco covered homes with tile roofs emulate the adobe Sonoran rowhomes of yesteryear. Saguaro cacti stand proudly in the front yards of these territorial and Spanish Colonial inspired homes. Prickly pears, yuccas, and ocotillo populate the backyards. You won't find the standard big-box retail appearance here, either: shopping centers are also designed to be one with the desert. Because of this, you can't blame the wildlife for being a bit confused and not knowing where the desert ends and neighborhoods begin. Coyotes, bobcats, road runners, and Gambrel's quail are some of the commonly seen visitors to the sprawling suburbs of Tucson. If a family of hairy pig-like creatures known as javelina happen to block your entrance into the local home improvement store, that is just fine — even worth a smile. And if an occasional mountain lion or bear passes through the neighborhood as they leave one mountain range and trek toward another, that's cause for bragging to your family or friends who live elsewhere in the country. And while these animals may captivate the locals, transients, and visitors alike, it is the other natives that make the visitors squirm: rattlesnakes, scorpions, Gila monsters, and tarantulas. Of course, few visitors actually ever see these residents, who like most of the region's wildlife would prefer to just be left alone.

The scenery around Tucson is among the most beautiful in the world, with local, state, and national parks beckoning one to enjoy this landscape up close and personal. The crystal clear cyan sky seems to go on forever, broken up only by mountain ranges and sky islands that provide an almost mystical backdrop, particularly when bathed in the crimson light of the rising or setting sun. Forests of saguaro personify the iconic image of the American Southwest, standing silently yet giving hints to their age based upon the number of arms reaching toward the endless sky. On the desert floor, arroyos entice plants and wildlife to dwell within their tranquil confines, only to change personalities with the arrival of the late summer monsoon rains, transforming into raging rivers.

Tucson is historic yet modern; sprawling yet quaint; desert yet mountainous. It is a melting pot of culture, where a diverse population of people live amongst an even more diverse population of wildlife. It is one of the fastest growing communities in the nation yet maintains its small-town charms. The Old Pueblo is in many ways one with its surroundings, which happen to be one of the most breathtaking settings to ever host a major metropolitan area.

Tucson: The Old Pueblo

View of Tucson from Sentinel Peak in the Tucson Mountains, with the Santa Catalina Mountains in the background. Tucson has many nicknames including the Old Pueblo, Optics Valley, the Sunshine Factory, and the City of the White Dove.

Founded in 1775 by Lt. Col. Hugo O'Conor, an Irishman serving in the Spanish Army, the fort known as Presidio San Agustín del Tucsón was located in what was to become Tucson. The eleven-acre fort was completed in the 1780s. Two corner towers stood twenty-feet in height, while the adobe fort walls stood between eight- and twelve-feet tall. In 1984, the Presidio Trust for Historic Preservation was founded to raise awareness of the region's Spanish and Mexican heritage and promote reconstruction of portions of the historic fort, which had been partially dismantled after the U.S. took control of Tucson in 1856 and was totally gone by 1918. In 1999, Tucson voters approved a ballot measure diverting tax money for reconstruction of the fort and other economic development initiatives. The northeast corner of the fort was built in 2007, offering residents and visitors alike the opportunity to travel to another era when Tucson was part of New Spain. In addition to a twenty-foot tower, or torreon, the fort includes a large mural depicting the portions of the fort that were not reconstructed.

Barrio Viejo is Tucson's oldest neighborhood and showcases a variety of adobe Sonoran rowhouses with colorful paint schemes. An early 1960s plan called for complete demolition of the neighborhood and relocation of over 5,000 residents. While that project was eventually abandoned, a smaller project was undertaken, resulting in the demolition of eighty acres of buildings and the relocation of 1,200 people to make way for the Tucson Community Center complex.

The historic Carrillo Elementary School was built in 1930 and named for Leopoldo Carrillo, a Mexican businessman. The prominent Mission Revival-designed school is one of the largest buildings in the Barrio Viejo neighborhood. In the 1870s, Carrillo constructed eight acres of gardens, orchards, and lakes nearby. Sadly, the Carrillo Gardens were demolished in 1925.

Barrio Viejo's El Tiradito is a shrine; it was added to the National Register of Historic Places in 1971. Translated as "The Castaway" and also known as the Wishing Shrine, El Tiradito is said to be the burial spot of a young man who found love with a married woman only to find death at the hands of her husband. For over 120 years, it has been maintained by Hispanic women who see it as an important destination for prayer and reflection. The historic site survived late 1960s plans for nearby development and early 1970s plans for construction of a new highway.

The Ferrin House was built in the 1860s and is one of the oldest adobe homes in the Barrio Viejo neighborhood. Today the building is home to the Cushing Street Bar & Restaurant.

La Pilita Museum is located on South Main Avenue. The building that houses the museum was constructed in the 1940s and served for many years as a restaurant. Today the museum features a collection of historic neighborhood photographs and oral histories as well as a gift shop. A number of educational programs are offered here. El Parquecito is the name of a small park located adjacent to La Pilita. At one time the site was home to the Sunshine Market as well as the entrance to Elysian Grove. Local residents constructed a fountain in the park atop an old well around 1980 and children from the surrounding community painted a large mural.

When it opened in 1915, Teatro Carmen was one of the only Tucson theaters dedicated to providing Spanish language entertainment. The theater was named for its founder, Carmen Soto Vasquez, and hosted operas, musicals, and literary productions until 1922. Afterward it became a movie theater, meeting hall, boxing venue, and an Elks Lodge.

Right:
The 23-story UniSource Energy Tower is the tallest building in Tucson. Previously known as the Norwest Tower, the steel and glass building incorporates copper colors of the desert with highly reflective black glass, creating a sparkling Post-modern skyscraper that complements the character of the surrounding neighborhood.

The Fox Tucson Theatre, opened in April 1930, was constructed for almost $300,000. The distinctive theater was designed by Eugene Durfee and built to host both vaudeville acts and talking pictures. The 1,200-seat theater was the largest in Tucson, and featured a stage and full fly loft; however, the dressing rooms were never completed due to the onset of the Great Depression. The theater eventually fell upon hard times and was closed in 1974. The Fox Tucson Theatre Foundation purchased the building in 1999, and a six-year, $13 million rehabilitation followed. The grand restored theater reopened on December 31, 2005. According the National Trust for Historic Preservation, the Fox Tucson Theatre is the only known example of a Southwestern Art Deco movie palace, combining Southwest territorial architecture with the Modern style popularized at the 1925 International Exposition of Modern Industrial and Decorative Art in Paris.

The Tucson Children's Museum opened in 1986 in a one-room building in Fort Lowell Park. Five years later the museum relocated to the former Carnegie Library, which offered 17,000 square feet of space for exhibits and programming. Today the museum is home to twelve permanent exhibits including Dinosaur World, Electri-City, Pet Vet, and Ocean Discovery Center. A $25,000 grant from Andrew Carnegie to Tucson was instrumental in allowing the former library building to be constructed; completed in 1901 from a design by local architect Henry Trost, the building featured a prominent dome that was destroyed in a 1941 fire.

Named for Father Francisco Garcés, a priest who accompanied Lt. Col. Hugo O'Conor on his mission to establish the Tucson presidio, this footbridge spans East Broadway Boulevard. Garcés served at the Mission San Xavier del Bac and explored much of Arizona, southern California, and Baja California. He was killed in a Quechan Indian attack at Mission San Pedro y San Pablo de Bicuner near present-day Bard, California. A nearby second footbridge is dedicated to Don Pedro de Allande y Saabedra, one of the first commanders of the presidio.

The colorful buildings of La Placita Village were designed to resemble a Mexican marketplace. Ten adobe and brick buildings house a number of offices, restaurants, and retailers. The site on which the complex stands was originally Plaza de la Mesilla when Tucson was part of Mexico. Later it was the location where wagon trains would depart for Mesilla, New Mexico or San Diego, California. The area came to be known as La Placita de San Agustin, or the Plaza of Saint Augustine, named for a nearby church that was later demolished when the congregation relocated to a new cathedral. The buildings of today were constructed in the 1970s.

The gazebo at Plaza de la Mesilla, or La Placita, is a replica of an 1880s period bandstand that stood in the plaza. The attractive structure has graced the plaza since 1955 and served as a backdrop for countless family photos, portraits, weddings, and performances.

15

The first Pima County Courthouse was constructed in 1868, four years after Pima County was established. More settlers began arriving, especially after completion of the Southern Pacific Railway to Tucson in 1880, and a larger courthouse was required. A picturesque Victorian building was completed in 1881 and operated until 1927. On the site of this second courthouse, a third Pima County Courthouse was built. Designed by architect Roy Place, the striking Spanish Colonial Revival building was constructed for a cost of $350,000. The brick building is clad in pink stucco walls while its massive cement dome is covered with sparkling ceramic tiles. The building's arches incorporate Moorish Revival overtones, a common feature southwest architecture. A large courtyard is surrounded on three sides by walls of the building and on the fourth side by an arcade or arched walkway. In 1974, a modern new courthouse was constructed to the south of the historic courthouse, which was added to the National Register of Historic Places in 1978.

The polychromatic dome of the historic Pima County Courthouse incorporates the hues of the surrounding desert, creating a glistening icon that helps define the Tucson skyline.

Before Tucson ever existed, even before the presidio was built, a small village by the name of San Agustín del Tucsón existed at the base of Sentinel Mountain. After the presidio was erected, a second village of the same name sprouted around it. Each of these villages had a church under the patronage of Saint Augustine. In the mid-nineteenth century, a church by the name of San Agustín Cathedral was built at the Plaza de la Mesilla. The congregation grew, and a new cathedral was constructed in 1897 on Stone Avenue in the Romanesque Revival style of architecture. The original design called for two front towers with spires reaching toward the heavens; however, due to cost constraints the spires were never constructed and the towers were squared off at roughly the same height of the center gable. In 1928, the building was given its current appearance, with a Mexican baroque façade inspired by the Cathedral of Querétaro in Mexico. The building was restored in the late 1960s, and today its façade exhibits a combination of religious and desert symbolism.

With a mission of "Connecting Art to Life," the Tucson Museum of Art has served the local community since it was established in 1924 as the Tucson Fine Arts Association. The museum relocated to a new Modernist building in 1975 and became steward for five adjacent historic properties. Permanent collections include Art of the American West, Art of Latin America, Modern and Contemporary Art, and Rare Books and Manuscripts.

This bronze sculpture, entitled "Yesterday is Tomorrow," is located in the eastside plaza of the Tucson Museum of Art. Created by California artist Betty Saletta, the sculpture has a twin located in Oakdale, California.

Looking through the Tucson Museum of Art's "Blue Arch" toward a colorful mosaic on the wall of the museum's Education Center.

The Joel D. Valdez Library opened in May 1990 and was renamed in 2003 for Valdez, who served as Tucson City Manager for sixteen years. The library has an annual circulation of 430,000 and receives approximately 700,000 annual visitors. It replaced the Carnegie Library on South 6th Avenue, which had served the residents of Tucson since 1901.

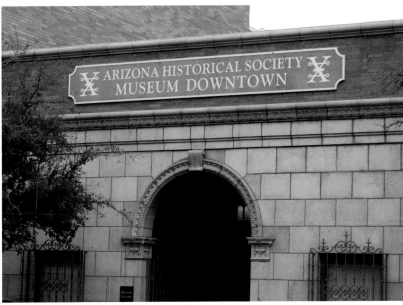

There are two Tucson museums of the Arizona Historical Society, including the Downtown History Museum. Located in the Wells Fargo bank building on North Stone Street, the museum includes exhibits that depict and interpret early life in Tucson.

A griffin is a legendary creature with the body of a lion, the head of an eagle, and the wings of a dragon or eagle. Tucson's very real griffin is a bright orange sculpture standing near the Scottish Rite Cathedral on Scott Avenue. In the early twentieth century, griffin sculptures stood atop the nearby Carnegie Library; however, they were removed in 1938. Known as "Toby," this metal griffin was produced by Creative Machines and installed as part of a 2009 streetscape enhancement project.

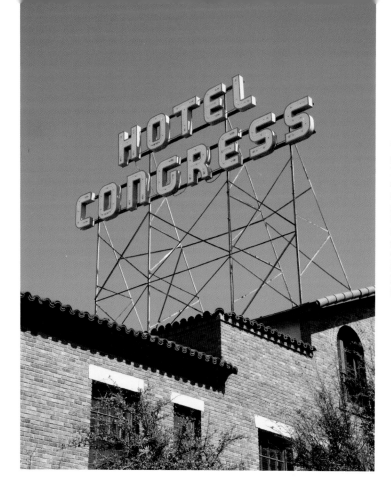

The famous Hotel Congress was built in 1919 and served railroad passengers, cattle-drivers, and other visitors. In 1934, John Dillinger and his gang hid out at the hotel, using aliases and lodging on the third floor. The hotel caught fire on January 22 and the gang offered to pay two firemen to retrieve their luggage. The firemen did retrieve the heavy bags — which were stuffed full of weapons and cash. Later, one of the firemen recognized the gang in *True Detective* magazine. He tipped off the Tucson Police, who were able to successfully accomplish what the FBI had not succeeded in doing: apprehending Public Enemy Number 1, John Dillinger. The building still operates as a historic hotel and is also home to the popular Club Congress.

Tucson is a city of murals, with several hundred colorful creations climbing the sides of concrete walls, underpasses, buildings, and columns. This prominent mural adorns the Radisson Hotel on West Broadway Street and depicts the arrival of the Spanish Conquistadors into Native American lands.

Tucson Music Hall is part of the Tucson Community Center complex that also includes the Tucson Convention Center and Leo Rich Theater. The concrete and block building was constructed in the late 1960s in an architectural style known as Brutalism. The performance theater holds over 2,200 people and regularly hosts Broadway in Tucson and the Tucson Symphony Orchestra.

Francisco "Pancho" Villa was a Mexican Revolutionary leader who was a general, bandit, and folk hero. The "Centaur of the North" helped overthrow Mexican Dictator Porfirio Diaz in 1910, but was also the leader of a ruthless band of outlaws known as "Villistas." He led a raid on Columbus, New Mexico in 1916. Though assassinated in 1923, Villa "returned" to the United States in 1981 — this time as a fourteen-foot, five-ton statue that was a gift from then Mexican President Jose Lopez Portillo to the people of Arizona.

El Presidio Park is a brick plaza located between the historic Pima Country Courthouse and City Hall. Situated on what was once the southern portion of Presidio San Agustín del Tucsón, the park today is home to shade trees, a large fountain, modern art, and veterans' memorials. It is a popular destination for workers on lunch break and the site of regular community events and festivals.

The Battle of the Bulge monument is located in El Presidio Park. Dedicated in 2003, the monument was funded solely by members of the Southern Arizona Chapter, Veterans of the Battle of the Bulge to honor those who fought in the late World War II battle that was the largest and bloodiest for American forces during the war.

During the Mexican-American War in 1846, Mormon soldiers entered Tucson on their way to California and hoisted the American flag over the community for the first time. The U.S. 101st Infantry Battalion, or Mormon Battalion, was organized in Iowa and marched 2,000 miles to San Diego. At the time, Tucson was part of Mexico and thus hostile territory; however, the occupation was peaceful, with opposing sides agreeing to barter instead of fight. Nervous citizens hosted a fiesta, and one of the soldiers entertained the local residents with his fiddle. This bronze statue in El Presidio Park commemorates the event.

Known as the Sosa-Carrillo-Frémont House, this adobe building is the last remnant of the barrio that was demolished for construction of the Tucson Community Center in 1971. The house was built in the 1870s; today it's a museum operated by the Arizona Historical Society — and a fine example of the Sonoran rowhouse that was once so prevalent in Tucson.

The towering Bank of America Plaza was constructed in 1977 and was Tucson's tallest building until construction of the Norwest (UniSource Energy) Tower.

Tucson's Temple of Music and Art is home to the Arizona Theatre Company, an organization founded in Tucson in 1967. Originally known as the Arizona Civic Theatre, the organization staged over two hundred plays during its first four decades of operation. The Temple of Music and Art was built in 1927 through the efforts of the Saturday Morning Music Club. The Spanish Colonial Revival building houses an art gallery, Temple Lounge, Cabaret Theatre, and the Alice Holsclaw Theatre, which seats 623 people.

A rich palette of colorful buildings line Scott Avenue, which received a major streetscape upgrade in 2009 as part of the City's Rio Nuevo project, a major downtown economic development initiative.

Trail Dust Town is said to have originated as a set for a Western movie starring Glenn Ford. Today it is a Western-themed attraction with the Pinnacle Peak Steakhouse, Savoy Opera House banquet facility, several retailers, a town square complete with gazebo, carousel, Wild West stunt shows, Museum of the Horse Soldier, and the CP Huntington Railroad.

The Tucson Convention Center was built in 1971 as part of the Tucson Community Center, which also included the adjacent Music Hall. As a portion of the Barrio Libre neighborhood was demolished to make way for the new complex, the project was controversial at the time. The convention center was expanded in 1989, adding more exhibit space and the familiar glass pyramidal skylights.

The Southern Pacific Railroad arrived in Tucson in 1880, connecting the town with Yuma. The original depot — where Wyatt Earp gunned down Frank Stilwell — was replaced in 1907 with a larger Spanish Colonial Revival station. Renovated and expanded in 1941, the train station lost much of its prominent architectural ornamentation in favor of the sleeker styling popular at the time. The depot, along with the adjacent buildings, were purchased in 1998 by the City of Tucson, and restored in 2004 to reflect its appearance of 1941. While rail service is still available at the historic station today, it is also home to offices, retail space, a restaurant, and a small museum.

The Southern Arizona Transportation Museum opened in 2005 in celebration of the 125th anniversary of the arrival of rail service in Tucson. Housed in the former Records Vault Building, the small museum offers exhibits that interpret the history of transportation in the region. A replica of the 1907 passenger station showcases the Spanish Colonial Revival appearance that largely disappeared in the 1941 renovation and expansion.

Southern Pacific Locomotive #1673 is located at the historic Train Depot on Toole Avenue. The coal burning locomotive was built in 1900 at the Schenectady Locomotive Works in New York. It logged over one million miles while in service, primarily as a freighter in southern Arizona. Locomotive #1673 made its Hollywood debut in the 1954 movie "Oklahoma," and one year later was retired and donated to the City of Tucson. It was moved to its current location in December 2000.

Downtown Tucson as viewed from Armory Park. The Children's Museum of Tucson is on the left.

Many historians believe that the Gunfight at the OK Corral is not the actual event that made Wyatt Earp and "Doc" Holliday legends of the American West. Rather, it was the events that occurred several months afterward. Earp and Holliday were arrested and tried for murder, but a judge declined to send them before a trial jury. Over the next few months, one of Earp's brothers was shot and another was murdered. Wyatt Earp, "Doc" Holliday, and several other men set out on what has become known as the Earp Vendetta Ride. The first adversary gunned down was Frank Stilwell, at the Tucson Train Depot, with Earp's Federal posse turning him into "the worst shot up man I ever saw," according to one eyewitness. Today, a statue of Earp and Holliday commemorates the event.

The modern Evo A. DeConcini United States Courthouse was dedicated in 2000, making it one of the newer buildings in downtown Tucson. At 413,000 square feet, it is also one of the largest. The building is a gateway between the city and the desert, incorporating flagstone, terracotta, stucco, concrete, and glass in a Post-modern fusion of building materials and architectural themes.

Picturesque Armory Park is located on the site of a Civil War-era camp and armory that operated from 1862 to 1873. Local residents were concerned about the occasionally rowdy behavior of the soldiers, necessitating relocation to the remote Fort Lowell northeast of town. Today the park is home to the Armory Park Center as well as several military-related monuments.

The El Paso & Southwestern Railroad had its beginnings as a 36-mile railroad for hauling copper from Bisbee to Fairbanks. In 1901, the Phelps Dodge Corp. founded the El Paso & Southwestern Railroad, expanding it to Tucson in 1912. The attractive Beaux Arts style depot was completed in 1913 and featured Indiana limestone columns and red Mexican roof tiles. Almost 3,000 Tucson residents turned out for the grand opening of the station and arrival of the first train. The building's life as a railroad station was short-lived, however: by 1924 rail traffic had all been diverted to the Southern Pacific Station and the building was abandoned. The El Paso & Southwest Railroad Station was added to the National Register of Historic Places in 2004.

The U.S. Federal Building on West Congress Street was constructed in 1974. Earth-toned concrete panels incorporate the color of the desert into a Modern Movement office tower elevated on four giant piers.

The Tucson Museum of Contemporary Art was established in 1997 and today occupies a former fire station. Its Brutalist Architecture fits with the museum's image as a home of modern and contemporary art. The 1973 concrete and glass building was designed by architect William Wilde and served as Fire Station No. 1 for over thirty-five years.

Founded in 1965, Reid Park Zoo is owned by the City of Tucson and features more than five hundred animals housed on seventeen acres. The zoo was created by and named for former Tucson parks and recreation director Gene Reid. It is defined by four zones: Adaptation Zone, South American Animals, Asian Animals, and African Animals. Visitors can enjoy a diversity of animal species including polar bear, gibbon, jaguar, lion, giraffe, and many more. Over 500,000 people annually visit the zoo, making it one of Tucson's most popular attractions.

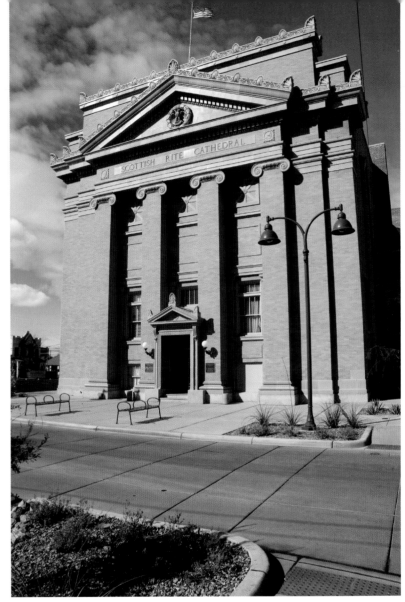

The Rialto Theatre was constructed in 1919-1920 by the same company that developed the Hotel Congress across the street. Named for a medieval-era covered bridge in Venice, the theater showed silent movies and hosted weekly vaudeville shows. The first full-length feature film shown here was The Toll Gate, which was written by and starred William Hart, a silent Western movie actor. The theater went through periods of success and challenge, eventually closing in 1984 after a boiler explosion. Eleven years later the Rialto Theatre was resurrected as a concert venue; today, managed by the non-profit Rialto Theatre Foundation, it is a preferred destination for concerts and events.

Scottish Rite Masonry in Tucson dates from 1875, when an organizational meeting was held. The cornerstone of the Tucson Scottish Rite Cathedral was laid in December 1915, and the building was dedicated the following year. The eclectic Neoclassical building, which includes Greek, Roman, and Egyptian architectural features, houses the Red Room, a large theater with seating for 350 people as well as large and small banquet rooms.

This view depicts El Presidio Park in the foreground and the Transamerica Building in the background. The latter was constructed in 1962.

Modernist architect William Wilde designed the Tucson Police Department in 1974. The massive building includes both a concrete structural frame and concrete panels, creating a "brutal" effect, and the architectural style is known as Brutalism.

The vibrant Tucson Visitor Center is located in the heart of the downtown, La Placita Village. Tourism is one of Tucson's major industries, with over 3.5 million visitors annually pumping in excess of $2 billion into the local economy.

This colorful sculpture, known as Sonora, was completed in 1991 by artist David Black and prominently stands in front of the Joel D. Valdez Main Library.

Eusebio Francesco Kino explored much of northwestern Mexico and southwestern United States, establishing twenty-four missions and vistas, or country chapels, including the Mission San Xavier del Bac south of Tucson. He was a missionary, author, astronomer, map-maker, and a key advocate for the Pima Indians. This West Alameda Street monument to Padre Kino was erected in 1936.

The Telles Block is today home to Old Town Artisans, an eclectic collection of shops and galleries. Located on the site of the original Presidio San Agustín del Tucsón, the adobe buildings that house the retail space were built in the mid-nineteenth century. An adjacent restaurant is located in a converted 1920s-era gas station.

The Wells Fargo bank building on North Stone Street incorporates an Italian Renaissance Revival style of architecture, with a two-story arcade featuring seven arches on each level. The building was constructed in 1955 for the First Interstate Bank.

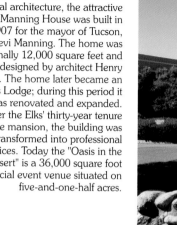

Described as Spanish Colonial Revival meets Santa Fe Territorial architecture, the attractive Manning House was built in 1907 for the mayor of Tucson, Levi Manning. The home was originally 12,000 square feet and was designed by architect Henry Trost. The home later became an Elks Lodge; during this period it was renovated and expanded. After the Elks' thirty-year tenure in the mansion, the building was transformed into professional offices. Today the "Oasis in the Desert" is a 36,000 square foot special event venue situated on five-and-one-half acres.

The Cheyney House on North Main Avenue was constructed in 1905 from a design by the architectural firm Holmes and Holmes. Though partially destroyed in a 1981 fire, a sympathetic 2001 restoration returned the Mission Revival style home to its original grandeur. The home was built for Annie Cheyney, widow of a notable local chemist and postmaster.

This handsome Mission Revival mansion, built in 1900 as the Owl's Club, was home to thirteen bachelors. The single men were all successful, and most eventually married. After the Owl's Club constructed a larger building nearby, the Henry Trost-designed building was purchased by Albert Steinfeld, owner of a Tucson department store.

DeGrazia Gallery in the Sun is the home and studio built by Ettore "Ted" DeGrazia, an acclaimed artist who lived from 1909 to 1982. After earning three degrees at the University of Arizona, DeGrazia furthered his art studies in Mexico City. Construction for Gallery of the Sun began in the 1950s with DeGrazia acting as architect and builder. His Mission of the Sun chapel was constructed in 1952. Today, the ten-acre property is a historic district listed on the National Register of Historic Places. Over 15,000 DeGrazia originals are housed at the Gallery of the Sun, which is maintained by the DeGrazia Foundation and open to the public for no admission charge.

Established in 1864, the Arizona Historical Society's mission is to collect, preserve, interpret, and disseminate the history of Arizona, the West, and northern Mexico as it pertains to Arizona. Museums are located in Tucson, Flagstaff, Tempe, and Yuma. The main museum in Tucson is located adjacent to the University of Arizona campus and focuses on southern Arizona history. Its main entrance is the salvaged portal from the San Augustine Cathedral, which was located at the Plaza de la Mesilla (La Placita) and demolished in 1936.

Established in 1893 as the Arizona Territorial Museum, the Arizona State Museum on the campus of the University of Arizona is the oldest and largest anthropology museum in the Southwestern United States. Today an affiliate of the Smithsonian Institute, the museum features both rotating and permanent exhibits, a library, an extensive collection and research materials, and a museum store. Permanent exhibits include Ancient Architecture of the Southwest, The Pottery Project, and Paths of Life: American Indians of the Southwest. The inviting red-brick building was designed by architect Roy Place and constructed in the 1920s as the University Library. Apache artist Craig Dan Goseyun created a bronze sculpture, Watercarrier, which stands near the front entrance of the museum.

When Old Main opened in 1891, it housed everything from offices to classrooms to sleeping quarters. The building, which features a Territorial architectural style, was the first campus building to be listed on the National Register of Historic Places. Today the building is home to the Office of Admissions and continues to be the centerpiece of the University of Arizona campus.

Completed in 1921, the University of Arizona's Maricopa Hall is the oldest residential hall on campus. The hall was originally planned as a two-story building; however, a third-story was added after the University changed architects. The distinguished building is still a residential hall for women, and is defined by a monumental Neo-classical portico with paired columns crowned by Egyptian capitals.

The University of Arizona's Flandrau Science Center was made possible through a bequest from the estate of Grace Flandrau, a noted author who published six novels and dozens of short stories between 1917 and 1943. The funds were used to construct the Grace H. Flandrau Planetarium, which opened in 1975 near the Steward Observatory and Lunar and Planetary Laboratory.

The Student Union Memorial Center on the campus of the University of Arizona prominently anchors the Mall. Completed in 2003, the building is approximately 400,000 square feet, making it one of the largest student union buildings in the nation. Over eight million pounds of steel were used to construct the building. The architect incorporated design themes from the *U.S.S. Arizona* Memorial at Pearl Harbor, with references to hulls, masts, bridges, and sails.

The area to the west of Old Main is today the West Campus Historic District, dating from the late nineteenth and early twentieth centuries. The area to the east of Old Main is known as East Mall. This "newer" section of the campus was laid out in 1931 by architect Roy Place with parallel roads separated by a large grassy area for use as a public space. The University's 119,000 square foot Integrated Learning Center, which opened in 2002, is located under the Mall.

Before coming to the University of Arizona to become director of the Lunar and Planetary Laboratory (LPL), Charles P. Sonnett was chief of sciences at the Lunar Programs Office of NASA. He was also heavily involved with ten NASA lunar experiments, including several Apollo missions. This noteworthy brick structure is named the Sonnett Space Sciences Building in his honor.

Arizona Wildcat Family is the name of a statue located on the University of Arizona Alumni Plaza. Tubac artist Nicholas Wilson created an enduring likeness of four bobcats — a male, a female, and two cubs — that was installed in 2004.

This sculpture of Hamlet was created by William Arms and presented to the University of Arizona's College of Fine Arts in 1996.

The Center for Creative Photography at the University of Arizona was founded in 1975. Ansel Adams, who is perhaps the most famous landscape photographer in history, helped establish the center. Today home to a 5,000-square-foot gallery, the Center for Creative Photography also houses The Institute for Photographic Research. Nearly 80,000 photographs, as well as 3.8 million archival items, are part of the collection, making it the largest institution of its kind.

The Tucson skyline as viewed from the barrio district.

Around Tucson

Designated a National Historic Landmark in 1960, Mission San Xavier del Bac is one of the most important examples of Spanish Colonial architecture in the United States. Father Eusebio Francisco Kino founded the mission in 1699. The original mission church was located several miles from the current building and was destroyed in a 1770 Apache attack. Though founded by Jesuits, the mission was overseen by Franciscans beginning in 1767. The mission building of today was completed in 1797 — fourteen years after construction commenced — and is located on the Tohono O'odham Reservation. Known as both the "White Dove of the Desert" and the "Sistine Chapel of North America," the mission annually hosts over 200,000 visitors.

The popular Arizona-Sonora Desert Museum was founded in 1952 and today annually hosts over a half-million visitors. Part natural history museum, part zoo, and part botanical garden, the museum seeks to inspire people to live in harmony with the natural world by fostering love, appreciation, and understanding of the Sonoran Desert. The 21-acre property comprises exhibits that house over three hundred animal species and more than 1200 plant species. Two miles of trails take visitors to see snakes, coyotes, mountain lions, Gila monsters, and much more.

If the saguaro is the iconic image of the American Southwest, and the only place to find a saguaro is the Sonoran Desert, then it stands to reason that Saguaro National Park is one of the best places to find a saguaro. To whit: according to the National Park Service, more than 1.6 million individual saguaro cacti grow within the park's boundaries. The 91,000-acre national park is actually split into two distinct areas: The Tucson Mountain District is located west of downtown Tucson and has a denser concentration of saguaros while the Rincon Mountain District is located east of the downtown and comprises a more diverse environment, rising from the desert floor to more than 8,000 feet above sea level.

The tallest point in the Santa Catalina Mountains is Mount Lemmon. Named for Sarah Lemmon, a botanist who climbed the mountain in 1881 with the help of Native American guides, the mountain reaches to a height of 9,157 feet above sea level, which is more than 6,700 feet above Tucson. The peak includes an astronomical observatory that was originally the site of a United States Air Force radar base; today the Mount Lemmon Station Observatory is operated by the University of Arizona. While Tucson may be recognized as one of the sunniest places in the United States, Mount Lemmon has a different climate, annually receiving as much as 180 inches of snow.

Opuntia, or prickly pear, is a common form of cacti found throughout the region. Resembling paddles with spines, and sometimes called the paddle cactus, prickly pears bear fruit known as the cactus fig that is consumed by javelina, coyotes, and desert tortoises and used in candies, jellies, and beverages for human consumption.

The Santa Rita Prickly Pear is known for its colorful violet pads and yellow or red blooms.

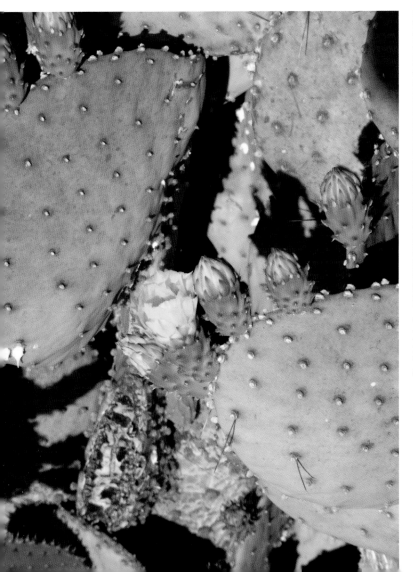

The Honey Bee Canyon Trail is located in the Oro Valley off of Rancho Vistoso Boulevard in Honey Bee Park. Snaking along a canyon floor, the trail is an important riparian area that provides great close-up views of mature saguaro cacti, a variety desert plant life, and desert wildlife like Gila woodpeckers, hawks, and even a solitary great horned owl.

For those of you who have never visited Old Tucson Studios, there is something immediately familiar about the place. Constructed in 1939 as a set for the movie "Arizona," the studio grew and expanded, becoming an iconic backdrop for many successful films including the original "3:10 to Yuma," "Gunfight at the O.K. Corral," "Rio Bravo," "El Dorado," "Joe Kidd," "The Outlaw Josey Wales," "Three Amigos," "Young Guns II," and "Tombstone," among countless other movies, TV shows, and commercials. Today this "Hollywood in the Desert" doubles as a theme park, offering shows, set tours, rides, dining, and shopping.

These Hohokam petroglyphs are located in Honey Bee Canyon in the Oro Valley. The Hohokam Indians lived in this area from around 450 AD to 1200 AD, so these glyphs may easily be a thousand years old or older. Note the figure of an owl on the right side of the boulder.

One of the Sonoran Desert's most commonly seen residents is the Gila woodpecker, a distinctive bird with white zebra striped back. If you haven't seen one of these birds, you've probably seen their homes: Gila woodpeckers excavate saguaro cacti to create cavities in which they nest. These cavities are known as boots.

The Palo Verde is the official state tree of Arizona. Its name translates as "green pole" or "green stick," a reference to the color of the tree's branches and trunk.

Standing north of Tucson, the Santa Catalina Mountains have the highest average elevation of the five mountain ranges that surround Tucson. Named in 1697 in honor of St. Catherine, the mountains are located within Coronado National Forest. The Santa Catalina Mountains are one of Arizona's "Sky Islands," so named because they are forested mountains isolated from one-another by "oceans" of desert and grasslands. According to the Sky Island Alliance, the Sky Islands region of the American Southwest covers 70,000 square miles of Arizona, New Mexico, and Mexico and features one of the most diverse ecosystems in the world.

To the west of downtown Tucson, Speedway Road turns into Gates Pass Road as it climbs through the Tucson Mountains and Tucson Mountain Park. The narrow winding road connects the city with popular attractions like Saguaro National Park, Arizona-Sonora Desert Museum, and Old Tucson Studios.

The mighty saguaro cactus is an iconic image of the American Southwest. A massive tree-like cactus, the saguaro can grow to heights of over fifty feet, reach weights of six tons, and live for over 150 years; in fact, many don't even grow their first arm until after the age of 50. Once a saguaro reaches the age of 35, flowers begin to grow, blooming at nighttime in April and May and remaining open for less than twenty-four hours. Saguaro fruit matures in June, providing a feeding source for birds, javelina, coyotes, and even humans. The plant's ribs were traditionally used as a building material by Native Americans.

Sentinel Peak, or the "A" Mountain, is located west of downtown Tucson. Part of the Tucson Mountains, it is named for the sentinels from the nearby presidio who would use the mountain as a lookout for approaching raiders. Students from the University of Arizona built the prominent "A" on the mountain in 1914 to celebrate an important football victory over Pomona College.

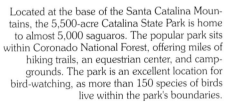

Located at the base of the Santa Catalina Mountains, the 5,500-acre Catalina State Park is home to almost 5,000 saguaros. The popular park sits within Coronado National Forest, offering miles of hiking trails, an equestrian center, and campgrounds. The park is an excellent location for bird-watching, as more than 150 species of birds live within the park's boundaries.

Despite its cuddly name, you wouldn't want to hug a teddy bear cholla. Found in the Sonoran desert at elevations up to 3,000 feet, this tree-like cactus grows to heights of six feet.

61

Selected as one of the world's great botanical gardens by *Travel + Leisure* magazine, Tohono Chul Park is a desert oasis located northwest of downtown Tucson. The park dates from 1966 when Richard and Jean Wilson began acquiring land. Despite offers from real estate developers, the Wilsons refused to allow their property to be developed for commercial use and, in 1979, they began turning it into a park, creating a path that grew into a loop trail. Tohono Chul Park was dedicated in 1985. In addition to the recognition from *Travel + Leisure*, the park was also selected by National Geographic Traveler as one of the Top 22 Secret Gardens in the United States and Canada.

The Sonoran Desert sits along the border of the United States and Mexico and covers portions of Arizona, California, Sonora, Baja California, and Baja California Sur. The 120,000 square mile desert contains several sub-regions, each with their own unique features and personalities. Tucson is located in the Arizona Uplands region. The Sonoran Desert is the only place in the world to find the iconic saguaro cactus, which has become the defining symbol of the American Southwest.

The Tortolita Mountains are one of five mountain ranges surrounding Tucson. Located north of Oro Valley, the mountains were once home to the Hohokam Indians. Honey Bee Village, remnants of a Hohokam village and ballcourt, is located in the foothills of the Tortolita Mountains as is Honey Bee Canyon, a popular hiking trail. Golf fans around the country know the Tortolita Mountains as the backdrop of the Jack Nicklaus-designed Ritz-Carlton Golf Club, Dove Mountain, location of the Accenture World Match Play Championship.

The golf courses around Tucson have produced some of the best professional golfers to play the game in recent years. Annika Sörenstam, Lorena Ochoa, and Jim Furyk all attended the University of Arizona. The rolling hills combined with the juxtaposition of nearby desert and towering mountains have created a golf destination known throughout the country. Pictured here is one of the newer golf courses in the region, The Preserve at Saddlebrook, which is nestled in the foothills of the Santa Catalina Mountains.

A colorful cactus blossom.

Catalina State Park takes on a different appearance at sunset as the desert landscape begins to bathe in the pastel colors of the fading light.

With the arrival of twilight, the most famous residents of the park, the saguaro cacti, transform into silhouetted sentries watching over the park and its nocturnal wildlife.

Beyond Tucson

In 1986, Space Biospheres Ventures began construction of the Biosphere 2 northeast of Tucson, near the Santa Catalina Mountains. Biosphere 1 is the planet Earth, and Biosphere 2 was built as a materially-closed ecological system. Two Human Missions were conducted here from 1991-1994. From 1996-2003, Columbia University managed the property; in July 2007, the University of Arizona assumed management of the structures and property. The original purpose of the facility was to understand how human sustainability could benefit from the natural creation of habitable conditions; research the effects of climate change; and investigate closed environments for future space colonization. Biosphere 2 contains recreations of five biomes found on earth. The facility comprises over 6,500 individual windows and 7.2 million cubic feet of sealed glass.

Located along the Santa Cruz River, Tubac is the site of the first Spanish garrison in what is today Arizona. It was the location of a presidio from 1752 to 1776, but after the presidio was relocated to Tucson, Tubac was left unprotected. This changed in 1787 when Spain reactivated the presidio and named it El Real Presidio de San Rafeal. The fort's foundations were excavated in 1974 and are now part of Tubac Presidio State Historic Park. Today Tubac is a well-known artists' colony with over eighty galleries and boutiques. In 2009, Yahoo Travel named Tubac one of America's Coolest Small Towns.

Tubac's El Presidito is a twentieth century building constructed to mimic a Spanish presidio. The building is home to several working artists and is located not far from the remnants of the original Presidio San Ignacio de Tubac, which was founded in 1752 after the small village of Tubac was destroyed during the Pima Revolt.

The Tohono O'odham Nation operates Tubac's Tohono Village Trading Post & Gift Shop. Here you'll find exquisitely crafted baskets, pottery, sculpture, paintings, and jewelry, created by Native American artists.

Once known simply as Complex 571-7, the Titan Missile Museum is today a National Historic Landmark south of Tucson. The Titan II Intercontinental Ballistic Missile (ICBM) played an important role in keeping the peace during the Cold War: the 9-megaton thermonuclear warhead could be launched underground from one of fifty-four locations across the U.S. and reach its target on the other side of the world in only thirty minutes. The complex is a popular tourist attraction where visitors can experience a simulated launch, view the 103-foot tall Titan Missile, and see the three-ton blast doors and eight-foot thick silo walls as they learn about Cold War technology.

In 1940, America lost one of its beloved movie stars when Tom Mix was killed in an accident north of Tucson on State Route 79. A star of over three hundred silent Westerns and early "talkies," Tom Mix is remembered as Hollywood's first Western megastar — blazing a trail followed by the likes of Ronald Reagan, John Wayne, and Clint Eastwood. Children across the country grew up watching Tom Mix movies on Saturday afternoons. Mix was so successful that Fox Film Corporation paid him $7,500 per week and constructed a Western movie set known as Mixville. His trusty sidekick was a horse named Tony. In 1929, Mix was pallbearer at the funeral of a true Western legend: Wyatt Earp. This memorial, located near the Tom Mix Wash on the Pinal Pioneer Expressway (SR-79), features a rider-less horse with its head bowed.

Casa Grande Ruins National Monument is located in Coolidge, north of Tucson. The property includes the ruins of several structures constructed by the Hohokam in the 1300s. The name Casa Grande is Spanish for "great house," an apt description for the remains of a four-story structure on the site. The Great House is sixty feet long and its four walls face the four cardinal points of the compass. Openings in the walls align with the sun and moon at certain times, including the summer solstice. In 1892, Casa Grande became the country's first archeological preserve and since 1932 the Great House has been protected under a roof covering.

Southeast of Tucson in Cochise County, where the Sonoran Desert transitions into the Chihuahuan Desert, sits the sun-baked town of Tombstone. Perhaps the most famous town of the Wild West, Tombstone was the site of an infamous street fight that pitted Wyatt Earp, his brothers Virgil and Morgan, and dentist-turned-gambler John Henry "Doc" Holliday against the McLaury and Clanton brothers. Known today as the Gunfight at the OK Corral, the event actually occurred on a vacant lot near the corral and on the street. Today, Tombstone is a major tourist attraction, annually visited by over 500,000 people.

After Cochise County was formed from Pima County in 1881, a new courthouse was required to establish a permanent location for conducting county business. This commanding Italianate building opened in 1882 and operated until the county seat relocated to Bisbee in 1929. Today the rehabilitated building, along with reconstructed gallows, is part of Tombstone Courthouse State Park. The Roman cross-shaped building houses a museum that interprets the history of Tombstone through exhibits, artifacts, and a replica of the original courtroom.

Cochise County's Mule Mountains rise to a height of 7,500 feet above sea level. Admist the natural skyscrapers sits a large man-made hole: the Lavender Pit. Named for a general manager of the Phelps Dodge Corporation, the open pit copper mine produced over 600,000 tons of copper, as well as gold, silver, and a type of turquoise known as Bisbee Blue. The mine operated from 1950 to 1974, covering an area of three hundred acres and reaching a depth of nine hundred feet.

Founded as a mining town in the Mule Mountains in 1880, Bisbee experienced rapid growth that coincided with the flooding of mines and decline of Tombstone. By the 1920s, the "Queen of the Copper Camps" was home to over 20,000 people. In 1929, the Cochise County seat relocated from Tombstone to Bisbee. Today, Bisbee is a regional center of culture and an eclectic artists' community with an impressive collection of Victorian architecture. Furthermore, Bisbee was once recognized by the AARP as being one of the "quirkiest" towns in America.

Bibliography

Online

"A Brief History of Arizona State Museum," University of Arizona, http://www.statemuseum.arizona.edu/about/history/index.shtml (accessed March 14, 2010).

"A Brief History of Mission San Xavier del Bac," http://www.sanxaviermission.org/History.html (accessed March 16, 2010).

"About Joel D. Valdez Main Library – History," http://www.library.pima.gov/locations/main/history.php (accessed March 17, 2010).

"About Southern Pacific Locomotive #1673," http://www.tucsonhistoricdepot.org/1673/about1673.htm (accessed March 17, 2010).

"About Tucson, Arizona," http://www.visittucson.org/visitor/about/ (accessed March 24, 2010).

"America's Coolest Small Towns," http://travel.yahoo.com/p-interests-29955069 (accessed March 20, 2010).

"Arizona Heritage Traveler – Historic Railroad & Depots – Southern Arizona Transportation Museum," http://www.arizonaheritagetraveler.com/templates/content-view.php?nid=2&sid=70 (accessed March 17, 2010).

"Arizona Superior Court in Pima County – History of the Superior Court," http://www.sc.pima.gov/Default.aspx?tabid=209 (accessed March 28, 2010).

"Arizona Theatre Company," http://www.aztheatreco.org/index.html?topbar.html&0 (accessed March 16, 2010).

Badertscher, Vera Marie, "Life Art: A Tour of Tubac, Arizona art Studios," http://www.pen4hire.com/html/tubac.html (accessed March 20, 2010).

"Bank of America Plaza," Emporis, http://www.emporis.com/application/?nav=building&id=127430 (accessed March 18, 2010).

Banks, Leo W. "The Return of Wyatt Earp," *Tucson Weekly*, April 22, 2004, http://www.tucsonweekly.com/tucson/the-return-of-wyatt-earp/Content?oid=1075940 (Accessed March 17, 2010).

"Barrio Viejo, Barrio Nuevo," *Tucson Weekly*, http://www.tucsonweekly.com/tucson/barrio-viejo-barrio-nuevo/Content?oid=1070273 (accessed March 14, 2010).

"Casa Grande Ruins National Monument (U.S. National Park Service)," http://www.nps.gov/cagr/index.htm (accessed March 23, 2010).

"Celebrating Tucson's Heritage," http://cms3.tucsonaz.gov/planning/prog_proj/projects/historic/pubandmaps.html#TopOfPage (accessed March 20, 2010).

Cheek, Lawrence W. "AmericanHeritage.com / TUCSON," http://www.americanheritage.com/articles/magazine/ah/2000/6/2000_6_76_print.shtml (accessed March 16, 2010).

"City of Tucson Parks and Recreation – Special Places 1," http://www.ci.tucson.az.us/parksandrec/specialplaces.php (accessed March 14, 2010).

Davis, Trista. "El Tiradito Shrine an Ode to Local Hispanic Folklore," *El Independiente*, October 23, 2009, http://www.elindenews.com/features/12-features/207-el-tiradito-shrine-an-ode-to-local-his (accessed March 14, 2020).

"Descriptions of Important Historic Sites," http://www.cdarc.org/pdf/scvnha/appendix_A.pdf (accessed March 17, 2010).

Devine, Dave. "The Other Station." *Tucson Weekly*, March 18, 2010, http://www.tucsonweekly.com/tucson/the-other-station/Content?oid=1872213 (accessed March 20, 2010).

"Downtown Tucson Partnership – Investment – Rio Nuevo," http://www.downtowntucson.org/investment/rionuevo/ (accessed March 21, 2010).

"El Paso and Southwestern Railroad Depot and Park – U.S. National Register of Historic Places on Waymarking.com," http://www.waymarking.com/waymarks/WM3E15 (accessed March 14, 2010).

"Exchange at the Presidio Marker," http://www.hmdb.org/marker.asp?marker=26443 (accessed March 14, 2010).

"Exhibitions – Arizona State Museum," Arizona State Museum, http://www.statemuseum.arizona.edu/exhibits/index.shtml (accessed March 14, 2010).

"Expeditions West: Tortolita Mountains, Tucson Arizona," http://www.expeditionswest.com/adventures/2004/tortolitas/index.html (accessed March 16, 2010).

"Explore Our Sky Islands," http://www.skyislandalliance.org/explore.htm (accessed March 21, 2010).

"Flandrau Science Center – Tucson Arizona Flandrau Planetarium," http://www.thepepper.com/tucson_flandrau_science.html (accessed March 17, 2010).

"Flandrau Science Center and Planetarium | The University of Arizona, Tucson, Arizona," http://www.arizona.edu/buildings/flandrau-science-center-and-planetarium (accessed March 17, 2010).

"Fox Tucson Theatre," http://www.preservationnation.org/resources/case-studies/ntcic/fox-tucson-theatre.html (accessed March 14, 2010).

Gassen, Sarah Garrecht. "Wildcat statue carries a UA message," http://www.uagrad.org/Plaza/wc_sclpt.shtml (accessed March 17, 2010).

"Gila Woodpecker Fact Sheet," http://www.desertmuseum.org/kids/oz/long-fact-sheets/Gila%20Woodpecker.php (accessed March 14, 2010).

Graeme, Jennifer L. "The Queen of the Copper Camps – Bisbee History," http://www.cityofbisbee.com/bisb_history.html (accessed March 19, 2010).

"Griffin Sculpture for downtown Tucson, AZ – Creative Machines," http://www.creativemachines.com/Public%20Art/Griffin/Griffin.html (accessed March 19, 2010).

Griffith, Joe. "In Pursuit of Pancho Villa, 1916-1917." http://www.hsgng.org/pages/pancho.htm (accessed March 14, 2010).

"Hamlet Visits the University of Arizona in Tucson," http://www.flickr.com/photos/ugardener/4388973275/ (accessed March 17, 2010).

"Hike Arizona: Honey Bee Canyon," http://hike-az.blogspot.com/2009/06/honey-bee-canyon.html (accessed March 16, 2010).

"History of the Fox Tucson Theatre," http://www.foxtucsontheatre.org/history/ (accessed March 14, 2010).

"Honey Bee Village," http://www.orovalleyaz.gov/Residents/culture_history/honeybee.htm (accessed March 16, 2010).

"Introduction," Barrio Historico Tucson, http://southwest.library.arizona.edu/barr/body.1_div.1.html (accessed March 15, 2010).

Johnson, Christopher. "Chapter 37. University of Arizona: Manuel Pacheco Integrated Learning Center | EDUCAUSE." http://www.educause.edu/learningspacesch37 (accessed March 20, 2010).

"Journey Into Tucson – Sunset.com," http://www.sunset.com/travel/southwest/journey-into-tucson-00400000017125/ (accessed March 15, 2010).

"Lunar and Planetary Laboratory | A Brief Overview of LPL," http://www.lpl.arizona.edu/history.php (accessed March 17, 2010).

"Maricopa Residence Hall | The University of Arizona, Tucson, Arizona," http://www.arizona.edu/buildings/maricopa-residence-hall (accessed March 17, 2010).

Marine, Matthew. "January 2008: Honey Bee Canyon." Arizona Highways, http://www.arizonahighways.com/static/index.cfm?contentID=1090 (accessed March 21, 2010).

Messina, Irene. "Pick – Tucson in Twilight." *Tucson Weekly*, June 2, 2005, http://www.tucsonweekly.com/tucson/pick/Content?oid=1080491 (accessed March 14, 2010).

"Mission and History :: Tucson Museum of Art :: 140 N. Main Avenue, Tucson, AZ 85701," http://www.tucsonmuseumofart.org/about/mission-history.php (accessed March 17, 2010).

"MOCA: Museum of Contemporary Art in Tucson, Arizona," http://www.moca-tucson.org/ (accessed March 14, 2010).

"Modern Architecture Preservation Project – Tucson, Arizona," http://mapptucson.org/ (accessed March 18, 2010).

"New Union Construction | Arizona student unions," http://www.union.arizona.edu/construction/ (accessed March 20, 2010).

"Old Pueblo, New Tucson | City of Tucson Web," http://cms3.tucsonaz.gov/history/about (accessed March 24, 2010).

"Padre-Eusebio-Francisco-Kino, S.J.," http://www.hmdb.org/marker.asp?marker=26394 (accessed March 15, 2010).

"Places in the Sun," http://parentseyes.arizona.edu/placesinthesun/maricopa.php (accessed March 20, 2010).

"Plaza de la Mesilla Marker," http://www.hmdb.org/marker.asp?marker=26432 (accessed March 19, 2010).

Popat, Mamta. "Focus on Tucson: Making a New UA Family." http://www.uagrad.org/Plaza/azstar.shtml (accessed March 17, 2010).

"Preservation," Cushing Street Bar & Restaurant, http://www.cushingstreet.com/Preservation.html (accessed March 14, 2010).

Prichard, Matt. "Tales from the Morgue: Bronze statue of Pancho Villa peacefully crosses border." http://elpasotimes.typepad.com/morgue/2008/12/bronze-statue-of-pancho-villa-peacefully-crosses-border.html (accessed March 14, 2010).

"Public Art – Tucson Pima Arts Council," http://www.tucson-pimaartscouncil3.org/dynamic/publicart/collection/collection.asp?cat=Mural&s= (accessed March 14, 2010).

Reel, James. "Rialto Redeux." *Downtown Tucsonan*, October 2004. http://www.downtowntucson.org/downtowntucsonan/oct04/vitalsigns.html (accessed March 15, 2010).

"ResLife: Maricopa Hall," http://www.life.arizona.edu/undergraduate/has/halldeSCRIPTs/maricopa.asp (accessed March 20, 2010).

"Rialto Theatre," http://www.rialtotheatre.com/PRINT_text.php?id=3 (accessed March 14, 2010).

"Rio Nuevo / Downtown | City of Tucson Web," http://cms3.tucsonaz.gov/rionuevo (accessed March 21, 2010).

Scoville, Ken. "Downtown's First Plazas." *Downtown Tucsonan*, March 2005. http://www.downtowntucson.org/downtowntucsonan/mar05/historic.html (Accessed March 19, 2010).

Simmons, Sam. "Family Hiking: The Honey Bee Canyon Trail." http://www.examiner.com/x-13492-Tucson-Outdoor-Recreation-Examiner~y2009m6d11-Family-Hiking-The-Honey-Bee-Canyon-Trail (accessed March 16, 2010).

"Southern Arizona Transportation Museum, Tucson," http://www.tucsonhistoricdepot.org/ (accessed March 17, 2010).

"St. Augustine Cathedral, Diocese of Tucson," http://www.diocesetucson.org/staug.html (accessed March 16, 2010).

"St. Augustine Cathedral – History," http://www.staugustinecathedral.com/history.html (accessed March 16, 2010).

Stiles, Lori. "LPL's July 20 open house celebrates lunar missions, birth of mission." http://uanews.org/node/2603 (accessed March 20, 2010).

"Student Union Memorial Center Grand Opening," http://www.union.arizona.edu/go/index.php (accessed March 20, 2010).

"Teatro Carmen Marker," http://www.hmdb.org/marker.asp?marker=26152 (accessed March 16, 2010).

"Temple of Music and Art Marker," http://www.hmdb.org/marker.asp?marker=26442 (accessed March 16, 2010).

"The Architect's Newspaper – MOCA Catches Fire," http://www.archpaper.com/e-board_rev.asp?News_ID=4323 (accessed March 14, 2010).

"The Arts in Tucson, Arizona," http://www.visittucson.org/visitor/attractions/arts/ (accessed March 14, 2010).

"The Buildings," http://jp.pima.gov/Pages/history/buildings.htm (accessed March 14, 2010).

"The Historic Hotel Congress – Tucson, AZ: Hotel History," http://www.hotelcongress.com/hotel-congress/hotel-history/ (accessed March 14, 2010).

"The Historic Manning House – Mansion History," http://www.manninghouse.com/mansion_history.htm (accessed March 14, 2010).

"The Preserve – Golf Club at Saddlebrooke," http://www.robson.com/page.cfm?name=SaddleBrk_Golf_preserve%20 (accessed March 15, 2010).

"The Steinfeld Mansion in Tucson Arizona," http://www.dotcomtucson.com/tucson_arizona_attractions/steinfeld_mansion.html (accessed March 14, 2010).

"The Tucson Murals Project: July 2008," http://tucsonmurals.blogspot.com/2008_07_01_archive.html (accessed March 21, 2010).

"The University of Arizona Alumni Association / Alumni Plaza," http://www.uagrad.org/Plaza/index.shtml (accessed March 17, 2010).

"The University of Arizona, Student Union Memorial Center and Bookstore – Project Details," http://schooldesigns.com/Project-Details.aspx?Project_ID=2462 (accessed March 17, 2010).

"Titan Missile Museum, The Front Line of the Cold War," http://www.titanmissilemuseum.org/ (accessed March 16, 2010).

"Tom Mix Death Site, Florence, Arizona," http://www.roadsideamerica.com/story/2425 (accessed March 16, 2010).

"Trail Dust Town," http://www.traildusttown.com/ (accessed March 16, 2010).

"Tubac Artist Colony – Tubac, Arizona – Arizona Tourism," http://www.arizonabeautiful.com/tucson-southern/tubac-artist-colony-tubac-arizona.html (accessed March 20, 2010).

"Tubac Chamber of Commerce | History of Tubac," http://www.tubacaz.com/abouttubac.asp (accessed March 16, 2010).

"Tubac Chamber of Commerce | Tubac Presidio State Park," http://www.tubacaz.com/presidio.asp (accessed March 16, 2010).

"Tucson Children's Museum – History," http://www.tucsonchildrensmuseum.org/index.php?option=com_content&view=article&id=78&Itemid=77 (accessed March 14, 2010).

"Tucson Daily Photo: 12' Tall Griffin Guards Tucson's Scott Avenue," http://www.tucsondailyphoto.com/2009/07/12-tall-griffin-guards-scott-avenue.html (accessed March 18, 2010).

"Tucson Historic Depot Home Page," http://dot.ci.tucson.az.us/depot/ (accessed March 20, 2010).

"Tucson historic year-round walk: points of interest along walk," http://home.att.net/~jdmount/tuhisptin.html (accessed March 19, 2010).

"Tucson Home Magazine: Design + Culture + Living – Artful Contemporary," http://www.tucsonhomemagazine.com/inthisissue/artfulcontemporary.html (accessed March 14, 2010).

"Tucson Newspapers: Media Kit," http://mediakit.tucson.com/mediakit.html (accessed March 27, 2010).

"Tucson Presidio Trust: About Us," http://www.tucsonpresidiotrust.org/about.html (accessed March 14, 2010).

"Tucson, Arizona Living, Tucson, Arizona Real Estate – Tucson Lifestyle Magazine," http://www.tucsonnewhomesguide.com/living.asp (accessed March 27, 2010).

"Tucson, AZ (TUS) – Great American Stations," http://greatamericanstations.com/Stations/TUS/Station_view (accessed March 20, 2010).

"Tucson's Barrio Libre," Barrio Historico Tucson, http://southwest.library.arizona.edu/barr/body.1_div.2.html (accessed March 15, 2010).

"Tucson's Public Art," http://www.tucson.halversen.com/art/native-mural.html (accessed March 21, 2010).

"University of Arizona, Comprehensive Campus Plan, Appendix 5: List of Historic Buildings," http://www.cfp.arizona.edu/files/Appendix%205.pdf (accessed March 20, 2010).

"Veterans of the Battle of the Bulge Chapter #53," http://history06.photos.military.com/gallery/2625317_gmaBd/2/141669695_y3sxQ/Small (accessed March 14, 2010).

"Welcome to Saletta Sculpture," http://www.salettasculpture.com/ (accessed March 20, 2010).

"Welcome to Tohono Village Trading Post & Gift Shop," http://www.tohonovillage.com/index.html (accessed March 19, 2010).

Wikipedia Contributors. "Biosphere 2." http://en.wikipedia.org/wiki/Biosphere_2 (accessed March 23, 2010).

"Cylindropuntia bigelovii." http://en.wikipedia.org/wiki/Cylindropuntia_bigelovii (accessed March 16, 2010).

"Eusebio Kino." http://en.wikipedia.org/wiki/Eusebio_Kino (accessed March 15, 2010).

"Frances Garces." http://en.wikipedia.org/wiki/Francisco_Garc%C3%A9s (accessed March 14, 2010).

"Mission San Xavier del Bac." http://en.wikipedia.org/wiki/Mission_San_Xavier_del_Bac (accessed March 16, 2010).

"National Register of Historic Places Listings in Pima County, Arizona." http://en.wikipedia.org/wiki/National_Register_of_Historic_Places_listings_in_Pima_County,_Arizona (accessed March 14, 2010).

"Opuntia." http://en.wikipedia.org/wiki/Prickly_pear (accessed March 16, 2010).

"Opuntia gosseliniana." http://en.wikipedia.org/wiki/Opuntia_gosseliniana (accessed March 16, 2010).

"Saguaro." http://en.wikipedia.org/wiki/Saguaro (accessed March 16, 2010).

"Santa Catalina Mountains." http://en.wikipedia.org/wiki/Santa_Catalina_Mountains (accessed March 17, 2010).

"Sentinel Peak (Arizona)." http://en.wikipedia.org/wiki/Sentinel_Peak_(Arizona) (accessed March 14, 2010).

"Tohono O'odham." http://en.wikipedia.org/wiki/Tohono_O%27odham (accessed March 15, 2010).

"Tom Mix." http://en.wikipedia.org/wiki/Tom_Mix (accessed March 15, 2010).

"Tortolita Mountains." http://en.wikipedia.org/wiki/Tortolita_Mountains (accessed March 16, 2010).

"Tubac, Arizona." http://en.wikipedia.org/wiki/Tubac,_Arizona (accessed March 20, 2010).

"Tucson Convention Center." http://en.wikipedia.org/wiki/Tucson_Convention_Center (accessed March 20, 2010).

"UniSource Energy Tower." http://en.wikipedia.org/wiki/UniSource_Energy_Tower (accessed March 17, 2010).

"University of Arizona." http://en.wikipedia.org/wiki/UniSource_Energy_Tower (accessed March 17, 2010).

"Wishing Shrine." Arizona Women's Heritage Trail, http://www.womensheritagetrail.org/women/WishingShrine.php (accessed March 14, 2010).

Books

Broyles, Bill. *Our Sonoran Desert*. Tucson, Arizona: Rio Nuevo Publishers, 2003.

Mitchell, David N. *The Insider's Arizona Guidebook*. Phoenix, Arizona: Arizona Highways, 2006.

Nequette, Anne M. and Jeffery, R. Brooks. *A Guide to Tucson Architecture*. Tucson, Arizona: University of Arizona Press, 2002.

Pamphlets and Unpublished Works

"Arizona-Sonora Desert Museum, self-guided tour map." Tucson, Arizona: Arizona-Sonora Desert Museum.

"Biosphere 2 – Tour Information." Tucson, Arizona: University of Arizona.

"Casa Grande Ruins." National Park Service, U.S. Department of the Interior.

"Center for Creative Photography." Tucson, Arizona: The University of Arizona.

Metropolitan Tucson Convention and Visitors Bureau, "Visit Tucson – Official Destination Guide, Spring/Summer 2010." Tucson, Arizona: Madden Media, 2008.

"Newcomers Guide 2009-2010." Tucson, Arizona: Tucson Home in Partnership with Metropolitan Tucson Convention and Visitors Bureau, 2010.

Office of External Relations and Arizona Student Media. "University of Arizona Visitor Guide, Spring/Summer 2010." Tucson, Arizona: University of Arizona, 2010.

"Old Town Artisans – Shopping & Dining." Tucson, Arizona: Old Town Artisans.

"Reid Park Zoo – Self Guided Tour." Tucson, Arizona: Reid Park Zoo / City of Tucson.

"The Presidio Trail – A Historical Walking Tour of Downtown Tucson." Tucson, Arizona: Tucson Presidio Trust for Historic Preservation, 2006.

"Tohono Chul Park – Map of Attractions." Tucson, Arizona: Tohono Chul Park.

"Your Complete Guide to the Parks." New York, New York: APN Media, LLC, 2009.